A Timeline of Food

Foraging to
Supermarkets

WORLD
BOOK

World Book
a Scott Fetzer company
Chicago

World Book, Inc.
180 North LaSalle Street
Suite 900
Chicago, Illinois 60601
USA

For information about other World Book publications, call 1-800-WORLDBK (967-5325).

For information about sales to schools and libraries, call 1-800-975-3250 (United States) or 1-800-837-5365 (Canada).

Produced for World Book, Inc. by Bailey Publishing Associates Ltd.

Library of Congress Cataloging-in-Publication Data

Title: Foraging to supermarkets: a timeline of food.
Description: Chicago: World Books, Inc., a Scott Fetzer company, 2016. | Series: A timeline of ... | Includes index.
Identifiers: LCCN 2016012913 | ISBN 9780716635475
Subjects: LCSH: Agriculture--History--Juvenile literature. | Food supply--History--Juvenile literature.
Classification: LCC TX355 .F664 2016 | DDC 630.9--dc23
LC record available at https://lccn.loc.gov/2016012913

Foraging to Supermarkets: A Timeline of Food
ISBN: 978-0-7166-3547-5
A Timeline of... Set ISBN: 978-0-7166-3539-0
E-book ISBN: 978-0-7166-3556-7 (ePUB3 format)

Printed in China by Shenzhen Wing King Tong Paper Products Co., Ltd., Guangdong Province
1st printing July 2016

Acknowledgments

Cover photo: Shutterstock (Liliya Shlapak).

Bridgeman Picture Library 11 (Musee des Antiquites Nationales), 13, 16 (De Agostini Picture Library), 17 right (Bibliotheque des Arts Decoratifs/Archives Charmet), 19 right (PVDE), 21 (Universal History Archive/UIG), 22 (Peter Newark American Pictures).

Corbis 4 top (Marilyn Angel Wynn/Nativestock Pictures), 7 left (David Cavagnaro/Visuals Unlimited), 8 left (Michael S. Yamashita), 10 (Jad Davenport/National Geographic Creative), 18 (Heritage Images), 19 left, 23 left (Bettmann), 24 left (National Archives-digital vers/Science Faction), 26 (Hulton-Deutsch Collection), 27 left (Hulton-Deutsch Collection), 28 (Charles Phelps Cushing), 29, 30 (Bettmann), 31 left (Bettmann).

culturedbeef.net 37 left (David Parry/PA Wire).

Getty 12 right (Alireza Firouzi), 20 (Archive Photos), 23 right (Sovfoto).

Shutterstock 4 bottom (1000 Words), 6 (MP cz), 7 right (I love photo), 9 top left (Diana Taliun), 9 bottom left (Masa44), 9 right (Attila Simo), 12 left (Makar), 14 (Martin Garnham), 17 left (Zilu8), 24 right (Gosphotodesign), 25 (SherSS), 27 right (Bogumil), 31 right (Stephen Coburn), 32 left (science photo), 32 right (Aleksey Stemmer), 33 (Thinglass), 35 left (Van Thanh Chuong), 35 right (Lightpoet), 36 (Stockr), 37 right (Everett Collection).

USDA Center for Nutrition Policy and Promotion (www.choosemyplate.gov) 34.

World Book 8 right, 15.

Staff

Writer: Cath Senker

Executive Committee

President
Jim O'Rourke

Vice President and Editor in Chief
Paul A. Kobasa

Vice President, Finance
Donald D. Keller

Vice President, Marketing
Jean Lin

Vice President, International
Kristin Norell

Director, Human Resources
Bev Ecker

Editorial

Manager, Annuals/Series Nonfiction
Christine Sullivan

Editor, Annuals/Series Nonfiction
Kendra Muntz

Manager, Sciences
Jeff De La Rosa

Editor, Sciences
Daniel Kenis

Administrative Assistant Annuals/Series Nonfiction
Ethel Matthews

Manager, Contracts & Compliance (Rights & Permissions)
Loranne K. Shields

Manager, Indexing Services
David Pofelski

Digital

Director, Digital Product Content Development
Emily Kline

Director, Digital Product Development
Erika Meller

Digital Product Manager
Lyndsie Manusos

Digital Product Coordinator
Matthew Werner

Manufacturing/Production

Manufacturing Manager
Sandra Johnson

Production/Technology Manager
Anne Fritzinger

Proofreader
Nathalie Strassheim

Graphics and Design

Senior Art Director
Tom Evans

Senior Designer
Matt Carrington

Media Editor
Rosalia Bledsoe

Manager, Cartographic Services
Wayne K. Pichler

Senior Cartographer
John M. Rejba

Special thanks to:

Roberta Bailey
Nicola Barber
Ian Winton
Alex Woolf

Glossary There is a glossary of terms on page 38. Terms defined in the glossary are in type that **looks like this** (called *boldface type*) on their first appearance on any *spread* (two facing pages).

Circa Some dates are written with *c.* before the year. The *c.* stands for *circa*. Circa means *approximately*. For example, with c. 250 B.C., the phrase is read as "circa 250 B.C.," meaning *approximately 250 B.C.* Circa can be used with both B.C. and A.D. dates.

Contents

Foraging to Supermarkets
A Timeline of Food

A selection of traditionally foraged foods, collected by the Hupa Indians, a native people of northwestern California in the United States.

Modern supermarkets offer a wide variety of packaged and fresh foods.

Introduction
Food and Farming Through the Ages

People need food and water to live. Food supplies the **nutrients** that the body needs to function. Today, people eat a variety of foods from both plant and animal sources. There are three main sources of food that give the body energy: *carbohydrates* (sugars and starches from such food as grains and fruits), *proteins* (from meats, fish, and beans), and *fats* (from many food sources). In addition to energy, fruits, vegetables, and dairy products provide the vitamins and minerals the body needs to stay healthy.

People have found and grown foods in different ways throughout time. Long before written history, humans were foragers, or hunter-gatherers. They hunted such wild animals as bison and caught fish from rivers and oceans. They also gathered fruits, nuts, seeds, and roots growing in nature. Around 9000 B.C., people started farming. The farming of plants and animals for human benefit is also known as **agriculture.** Farmers settled in one location to plant crops and raise animals to eat. Villages, cities, and eventually, great civilizations were developed around food sources.

Farming methods have changed greatly over time. Today, agricultural machines do much of the work that human farmers used to do by hand. With new technology and scientific knowledge, farms in **developed countries** produce far more food today than ever before. But modern farming practices can cause damage to the **environment.** In less developed countries, many people work as farmers, but some struggle to grow enough food to feed their community or themselves. Even though farmers produce huge amounts of food, millions of people still go hungry.

To learn more, follow the timeline through this book and trace the history of food and farming practices from the earliest civilizations to the present day.

Chapter 1

The Origins of Farming
c. 9000 B.C.—c. 4000 B.C.

Before farming, people found their food by hunting animals and gathering plants. Small groups of such hunter-gatherers moved around from place to place to find food to eat. This method is called *foraging*. Around 9000 B.C., people in the region of the world known as the Middle East took the first steps towards becoming farmers. In an area called the *Fertile Crescent,* in what is now Iraq and Syria, people picked seeds from the biggest and tastiest plants. By planting these seeds, such food plants as barley and wheat became bigger and tastier over time.

People in China domesticated rice. The Chinese were also the first to raise pigs and chickens.

People in the Andes Mountains in South America domesticated the vegetable we call squash. Later, they grew lima beans, peanuts, and potatoes. They kept guinea pigs and llamas as livestock.

People in New Guinea, a large island in the Pacific Ocean, north of Australia, possibly domesticated two potatolike crops—the yam and the taro—by 7000 B.C. They may have also been the first to domesticate bananas and sugar cane.

c. 8000 B.C.

8000 B.C.

c. 9000 B.C.

People in the Fertile Crescent began domesticating wheat, barley, and peas.

7000 B.C.

People in China, South and Central America, and the large island of New Guinea in the Pacific Ocean also **domesticated** wild plants. The process of domestication changes wild plants into varieties that can be more easily farmed. The most important plants on ancient farms were grasses with seed grains, including barley, corn, rice, and wheat. These grains became **staple crops.** Starchy tubers, such as potatoes, were other important staple crops. Early farmers also domesticated such livestock animals as cattle, chickens, and goats. They tamed and bred wild animals to raise for their meat, eggs, and milk.

Farming spread quickly from these centers of domestication. Instead of moving to seek food, farmers could grow their food in the same place year after year. They were able to build villages around the farms that later developed into large cities.

Painted pottery from Mesopotamia, a land in the Fertile Crescent, shows scenes of workers fermenting foods. Fermentation was an important way to **preserve** food in the ancient world. In fermentation, people let such helpful microbes as **bacteria** and yeasts grow on food. These microbes help keep harmful microbes away. New food flavors, and sometimes alcohol, are products of fermentation. Fermented foods last a long time. The Mesopotamians made bread and beer from fermented grains. Fermentation processes continue to be used today to make such foods as cheese and yogurt.

c. 4200 B.C.

c. 4000 B.C.

In areas of what is now the country of Mexico, people domesticated the corn plant (right) from its wild ancestor, called *teosinte* (left).

Ancient Farmers
c. 3300 B.C.—A.D. 200's

All crops need water. Most crops grow best on flat land. To meet these needs, early farmers changed the shape of the land around them. In ancient Mesopotamia, Sumerian farmers built **irrigation** systems to supply needed water. Mesopotamia was located in the Fertile Crescent, between the Tigris and Euphrates rivers. Rain is rare in this region. Farmers dug canals from the rivers to their farmland. By forming canals, their crops received a steady supply of water, even without rain. The ancient Egyptians also used irrigation canals.

The people of Sumer in Mesopotamia built the first cities beginning about 3300 B.C. People living in such early cities were supported by nearby farms. To irrigate their crops, Sumerian farmers built canals to bring water from the Tigris and Euphrates rivers. A *ziggurat* (a stepped pyramid-shaped temple) was usually built in the center of a city. The ruins of one ziggurat built in the Sumerian city of Ur in about 2050 B.C. (above) still stand in the modern country of Iraq.

c. 3300 B.C.

3100 B.C.

The Egyptians built their first major irrigation system.

Farmers in hilly areas cut steplike terraces into the slopes. The terraces collected rainfall that would have otherwise run down the hillside. The Chinese grew rice on terraced slopes as early as 5000 B.C. The terraces allowed farmers to grow rice in flooded sections, called *paddies,* without the water running down the slope.

Early farmers used tools called *plows* to help plant crops. This agricultural tool is used to turn over soil and create straight rows in which to plant seeds. The first plows were likely made from branched tree sticks. Beginning in the 3000's B.C., the ancient Sumerians and Egyptians attached plows to powerful animals called *oxen.* Much later, people learned to make plows out of metals called *bronze* and *iron.* Improvements to the plow continued for thousands of years. It is still one of the most important farming tools used today.

The Egyptians used grapes to make wine.

Black pepper, cinnamon, and cumin are spices grown on plants. Spices give foods flavor. In ancient times, spices were rare foods. These three spice plants grew well in Asia. But people in Europe and the Middle East also wanted to use these spices. To get spices, some people became sea traders. They sailed by ship to buy and sell spices among continents. For example, the ancient Greeks and Romans paid much money for black pepper grown in what is now India. Much later, the spice trade became a huge business.

2500 B.C.

c. 2000 B.C.

2600 B.C.

People in the Indus Valley, in what is now Pakistan, had developed cities with irrigated farms.

Cinnamon

Cumin

Black pepper

Ancient Farmers
c. 3300 B.C.—A.D. 200's

The first farming communities sometimes grew more food than they needed to eat. Farmers could trade the extra crops or livestock with other people. Some people in the community could work different jobs on the farms in exchange for food. Other people became builders, bakers, warriors, or writers. Some people in the city grew wealthier and more powerful than others. In many ways, ancient civilizations were built around the ability of farmers to grow enough food to support the people living in the surrounding areas.

The Indus Valley civilization had disappeared after hundreds of years of decline. Scholars believe the Indus Valley people may have overused their farmland, causing **environmental** damage. People likely moved away from this land in search of better food sources.

c. 1700 B.C.

c. 1200 B.C.

Many ancient civilizations in the Middle East suffered through serious **drought** and **famine.** Invaders also put pressure on these civilizations. Great cities in ancient Egypt, Mesopotamia, and Greece fell into ruin, marking the end of the Bronze Age. The Bronze Age was a period when tools and weapons, including farming plows, were made out of the metal bronze.

c. 900 B.C.

The Maya, who lived in areas of what is now Mexico and Central America, grew cacao. Cacao is a bean used to make chocolate. The Maya collected the beans and dried them in the sun, then roasted and ground them. They mixed the cacao powder with hot water and added such flavorings as chilies and vanilla to make a chocolate drink. The Olmec, an earlier group of peoples who lived in the same areas, may have grown cacao even earlier.

Over time, farmers developed better farming tools and methods. For example, the ancient Romans developed **crop rotation** around 500 B.C. Instead of growing the same crop on the same piece of land every year, they switched between raising two different crops. Some farmers also left parts of their fields empty each planting season. These practices helped the soil stay healthy over many years. Crop rotation methods quickly spread throughout Europe.

By the 200's B.C., the ancient Romans had built a complex **irrigation** system with canals and *aqueducts* (channels made to transport water). Around the same time, people in China invented a new agricultural tool called the *water wheel.* It used the power of moving water to grind grains into small pieces to use in cooking.

The Chinese started to practice aquaculture. This method of raising fish for food, instead of catching them in the wild, can help ensure enough food is available for a whole community.

c. 500 B.C.

100's B.C.

In China, under the Han dynasty (206 B.C. to A.D. 220), the water wheel was invented. This device used the power of flowing water to power water mills. A mill is a machine that grinds grains. The motion of the flowing water spun the wheel and powered a type of hammer. The hammer pounded grain to remove the *husk* (dry outer part).

A.D.100's–A.D. 200's

In the ancient Roman Empire (at its peak in the A.D. 100's and A.D. 200's), the most important crop was wheat. People learned to make bread from this grain. Romans also grew many types of apples. Due to the great size of the Roman Empire, bread baking methods and apple varieties spread to many parts of Europe.

Developments in Food and Trade
A.D. 350—Late 1400's

In western Europe, the **Middle Ages** began when the Roman Empire fell in the A.D. 400's. By the A.D. 800's, most of western Europe was divided into large areas of land called *manors.* A few wealthy landowners, called *landlords* or *lords,* ruled the manors. Each village on a manor produced nearly everything needed by its people. *Peasants* (a type farmer who lived on and worked the manor's land; sometimes called *serfs*) were employed by the landlord. The peasants gave part of their crops to the lord. In return, the landlord protected them from enemies.

The earliest known mention of tea appeared in early Chinese literature. According to legend, the method of using plant leaves to make tea had been discovered thousands of years earlier.

A.D. 350

A.D. 400's

The Chinese used a harness to allow horses to plow fields quickly.

A.D. 600's

Windmills were invented in Persia, in what is now the country of Iran. Early windmills were used for grinding grain. Later, they were used to pump water, and today they produce electric power.

In years when crops grew well, the peasants could give up part of their food supply and still keep food for themselves. But if crops grew poorly, the peasants sometimes went short of food. This system was called *manorialism.*

In China, farmers learned how to use a harness to connect a plow to a horse. Horses could drag plows faster and for a longer period of time than oxen could. The horse harness was later introduced to farmers in Europe and is still used on farms in many parts of the world.

Agriculture in North and South America developed independently from agriculture in Europe, Africa, and Asia. Some Native Americans formed great cities and empires. Farmers in the Americas focused more on growing crops than livestock.

During the Song Dynasty (A.D. 960-1279) in China, farmers began to use early-ripening rice. This type of rice could produce two or three harvests each year. The increase in crops helped to support a rapid growth in China's population.

A.D. 960

c. A.D. 900

The Maya civilization began to decline. Crop failures and environmental damage may have caused the decline.

Developments in Food and Trade

A.D. 350—Late 1400's

The Inca and other western South American peoples lived in the cold Andes mountains. They learned to freeze-dry meats and potatoes. Then they stored the dried foods to eat later. *Jerky,* the word for dried strips of meat, comes from the Quechua language of the Inca.

Trade and conquest helped to spread many foods and spices around the world. Many spices grew in Southeast Asia, particularly the Spice Islands of Indonesia in the Indian Ocean. Like the ancient Romans and Greeks, many Europeans valued such spices as black pepper and cinnamon. Rival empires controlled the

The city of Venice, in the northern part of what is now Italy, became the major trading power in the eastern Mediterranean Sea. The city was the hub of the spice trade between Europe and Asia.

1380

1100's

The Islamic Empire (A.D. 600's to 1200's), based in the Middle East, introduced lemons to Spain. At this time, the Islamic Empire stretched from north Africa to India and included Spain. Many now-common European foods, including eggplants, artichokes, and sugar, were originally introduced to the region during the empire's rule.

1200's

Coffee beans were brought to Arabia (now Saudi Arabia) from Africa. According to legend, coffee was originally discovered in what is now Ethiopia when goat herders noticed that their flocks stayed awake all night after feeding on coffee leaves and berries.

trade routes between Europe and the Spice Islands. To **import** spices by land, Europeans had to pay taxes and fees.

The desire for spices encouraged exploration throughout the world. Reaching the Spice Islands by sea was not easy for European sailors. To get to the islands, they sailed around the southernmost point of Africa, a voyage that took weeks. Europeans wanted to find new sailing routes to the Spice Islands. In the 1490's, the rival countries of Spain and Portugal funded different explorers to chart new ocean routes. But instead of finding the islands, some Europeans sailed across the Atlantic Ocean and unexpectedly came upon the continents of North and South America. The explorers found farmers in the "New World" raising different kinds of crops and livestock than those of European farmers.

1492

Christopher Columbus (1451-1506) sailed from Europe to the Caribbean Islands. His voyage was supposed to find a quicker sea route to Asia. Instead, Columbus encountered a "New World." Columbus brought back corn, chili peppers, and turkeys to Europe. The following year, Columbus planted the first fruit trees and sugar cane plants in the Caribbean Islands. Over time, many types of foods were exchanged among countries.

King Manuel I of Portugal (1469-1521) funded sea captain Vasco da Gama (1469?-1524) to find a new route to the Spice Islands. Da Gama sailed all the way around southern Africa to reach his destination.

1498

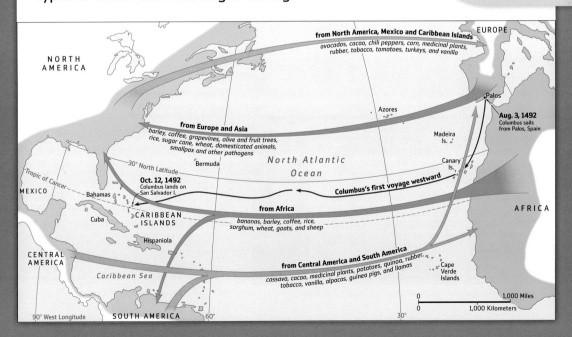

from North America, Mexico and Caribbean Islands
avocados, cacao, chili peppers, corn, medicinal plants, rubber, tobacco, tomatoes, turkeys, and vanilla

EUROPE

NORTH AMERICA

from Europe and Asia
barley, coffee, grapevines, olive and fruit trees, rice, sugar cane, wheat, domesticated animals, smallpox and other pathogens

Azores

Madeira Is.

Palos

Aug. 3, 1492
Columbus sails from Palos, Spain

Bermuda

Canary Is.

North Atlantic Ocean

30° North Latitude

Tropic of Cancer

MEXICO

Oct. 12, 1492
Columbus lands on San Salvador I.

Bahamas

Columbus's first voyage westward

Cuba

CARIBBEAN ISLANDS

from Africa
bananas, barley, coffee, rice, sorghum, wheat, goats, and sheep

AFRICA

Hispaniola

CENTRAL AMERICA

Caribbean Sea

from Central America and South America
cassava, cacao, medicinal plants, potatoes, quinoa, rubber, tobacco, vanilla, alpacas, guinea pigs, and llamas

Cape Verde Islands

0   1,000 Miles
0   1,000 Kilometers

90° West Longitude   SOUTH AMERICA   60°   30°

Chapter 4

Old and New Worlds
1500's—1760's

After Christopher Columbus arrived in the Americas, **agriculture** became truly global for the first time in history. Before 1492, people in Europe, Asia, and Africa—the "Old World"—had never tasted vanilla, chocolate, tomatoes, potatoes, or chili peppers. These foods had grown only in the Americas, the "New World." For Native Americans, foods from Europe, Asia, and Africa were just as new. Native Americans had never seen wheat, rice, onions, or garlic. Such livestock animals as horses, cattle, or chickens were also new to Native American peoples.

Portugal paid Spain for the rights to control trade on the Spice Islands, ending the conflict between the two powers. Before this time, Spain and Portugal fought to control the sea trade routes.

1529

Tobacco was a very important New World crop used to make medicines, cigarettes, and cigars. The Portuguese set up tobacco and sugar plantations in Brazil. Spain, Portugal's rival, built similar plantations on islands in the Caribbean Sea.

1500's

The exchange of crops and livestock among these continents greatly changed agricultural practices around the world. Europeans started to conquer land and settle in the Americas. They brought horses and farming tools with wheels, which Native Americans had never before used. Soon, people in the Americas were farming such Old World crops as wheat and onions alongside such New World **staple crops** as corn and squash.

Europeans also brought New World crops back to the Old World. For example, Portuguese and Spanish traders carried hot chili peppers from Mexico to such places as North Africa, India, Thailand, and China. As they became more commonplace, spicy peppers were an important ingredient in many traditional Old World *cuisines* (foods and cooking methods of a particular region).

1548

European explorers brought tomatoes to Italy from South America. Over the next 300 years, farmers in Italy gradually accepted tomatoes into their **crop rotations.** However, many popular tomato-based Italian dishes, such as pizza and pasta sauce, were not cooked until the 1800's.

c. 1570

Spanish explorers brought potatoes to Europe from South America. Potatoes became an important staple food in many places, especially Ireland.

Old and New Worlds
1500's—1760's

In both North and South America during this period, food production on a large scale began. In the early 1500's, European settlers living in warm areas established huge farms called *plantations.* They raised cocoa beans, cotton, sugar cane, and tobacco—crops that grow well in warm, humid climates. Many of these crops were **exported.** The plantations needed many workers to farm the large plots of land. At this time, the cruel practice of slavery was legal. Slave traders began to capture and enslave west African people to be sold to European settlers to work on their plantations in the Americas.

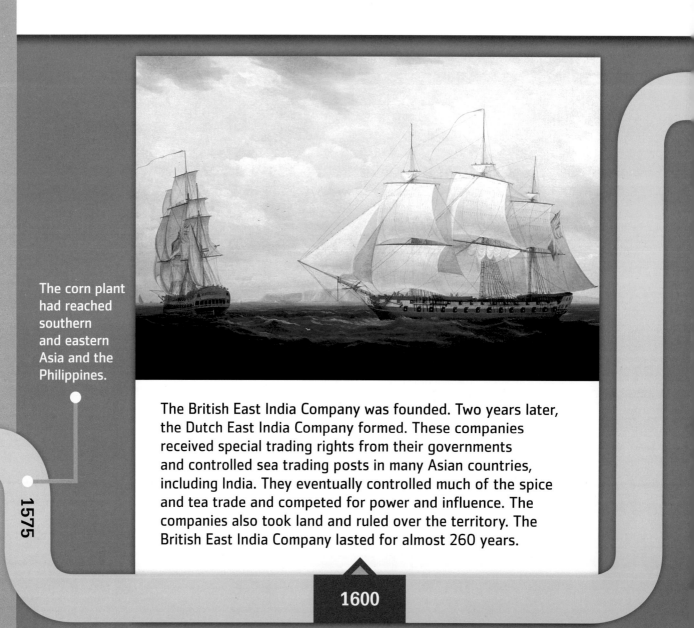

The corn plant had reached southern and eastern Asia and the Philippines.

1575

The British East India Company was founded. Two years later, the Dutch East India Company formed. These companies received special trading rights from their governments and controlled sea trading posts in many Asian countries, including India. They eventually controlled much of the spice and tea trade and competed for power and influence. The companies also took land and ruled over the territory. The British East India Company lasted for almost 260 years.

1600

When European settlers traveled across the Atlantic Ocean, they arrived in the eastern portion of North and South America. To find more open land, the settlers moved westward, sometimes taking Native American lands. In some places, Native Americans worked on European farms in return for food or wages. In other areas, displaced Native Americans struggled to grow or hunt enough food to survive.

In the mid-1700's, Italian priest and scientist Lazzaro Spallanzani invented an early method of **preserving** food called *canning.* This major advance in food preservation involves cooking food sealed inside of glass jars or metal cans to kill the **bacteria** that causes it to spoil. This preservation method allows food to be stored for a long time without going bad.

1600's

Coffee beans were taken from Turkey to Italy. Europeans began drinking the beverage in coffee houses, which became popular meeting places. In the 1660's, coffee probably arrived in the American colonies along with European settlers.

1760's

Lazzaro Spallanzani (1729-1799) sealed broth, a thin soup, in glass jars and boiled the jar to preserve the food inside. He showed that no living things grew inside the jars as long as they stayed tightly sealed. His work formed the basis of canning foods for long-term storage.

Chapter 5

Agriculture and the Industrial Revolution
1765—Late 1800's

In Europe, improvements in **agricultural** practices and tools meant that fewer people were needed to work the land. More people moved to cities, where they found work in new factories. This movement of laborers helped lead to the Industrial Revolution in the late 1700's and 1800's. This movement caused a great change in society and technology. Factories ran on new steam-powered machines.

The first restaurant opened in Paris, France. Diners could order a meal from a menu with various choices. With this new type of business, many people were able to become professional cooks, or chefs. Later, cooking schools opened to teach students how to prepare many types of foods.

American inventor Eli Whitney (1765-1825) invented a new cotton gin. Whitney's machine greatly influenced cotton production in the southern United States. Whitney's machine could clean the same amount of cotton in one day as that of 50 people working by hand. This invention made cotton a valuable crop and increased the need for field laborers on plantations. Cotton fibers were woven into soft fabrics to make clothing, bedsheets, and other items, as they still are today.

1765

1794

Workers produced many goods cheaply and quickly, including farming tools.

Eventually, the technology of the Industrial Revolution influenced farming techniques throughout the United States and Europe. Improvements included steam-powered farm machinery and new **fertilizers.** At the same time, American inventor Eli Whitney improved the cotton gin. A cotton gin is a machine that removes the seeds from cotton fibers. This new machine made picking cotton more profitable and increased the demand for slaves to work on American farms. Throughout the 1700's and the first half of the 1800's, millions of Africans were taken to labor as slaves on the plantations in the Americas. Cotton soon became the leading crop in the United States.

American tool designer Cyrus Hall McCormick (1809-1884) patented his design for the mechanical reaper. This machine helped to harvest grains faster. As horses pulled the reaper across the field, the machine sawed through tall stalks of grain. Workers gathered the stalks and tied them into bundles. The design was later improved so fewer workers were needed.

1812

1834

French chef Nicolas Appert (1749-1841) built upon Lazzaro Spallanzani's canning method. Appert learned how to **preserve** soup, fruit, vegetables, and dairy products in sealed glass containers. He published his findings, which helped lead to the widespread canning of food for sale.

Agriculture and the Industrial Revolution
1765—Late 1800's

During the 1800's, new tools and technologies made farming in northern regions of the world easier. A new type of plow made of steel could cut through the heavy soil of North American prairies. A new reaping machine, for cutting and collecting crops, worked much faster than farmers cutting stalks by hand. To store large harvests, farmers built grain elevators on their property.

Until the late 1800's, farm machinery was still pulled by horses, donkeys, or other animals. The first steam-powered tractors were invented in the 1870's, but they did not work very well. The tractors could lift objects above the ground but

1837

American inventor John Deere (1804-1886) created the steel plow. Steel is a strong, flexible metal material. When pulled by horses, the steel plow could cut through the heavy, sticky soil of North American prairies. The steel plow is still a valuable tool on many modern farms.

American inventor Joseph Dart (1799-1879) built the first steam-powered grain elevator in Buffalo, New York. Huge buckets scooped up grain and raised it to a large wooden tower. Then, the grain was placed in tall bins for storage.

1842   **1862**

The United States government established the Department of Agriculture (USDA). In 1899, it became a cabinet-level department. Originally this organization helped increase food production. Today the organization helps support farmers' incomes, ensures food safety, and works to fight hunger. Other **developed countries** have similar organizations.

could not move backwards and forwards easily. Later, gasoline-powered tractors replaced steam tractors. These improved tractors could move freely, dragging large planting and reaping machines behind them.

New forms of transportation also improved farming methods. Steam-powered railroads became common, first in the United Kingdom and then in the United States. With railroads, farmers could quickly transport their crops from one region to another, increasing sales and profits. Railroads also carried tools, seeds, and other supplies farmers needed to work the land. By the early 1800's, such fresh foods as meats could be packed in refrigerated train compartments. These cooled compartments helped farmers ship foods to customers thousands of miles away.

The American Civil War (1861-1865) ended. Black slaves on southern plantations were freed. Many former slaves became sharecroppers. They rented farmland from wealthy landowners and gave a portion of the crops they grew to the landlord.

1865

Austrian monk Gregor Mendel (1822-1884) published research that showed that animals and plants pass on features to *offspring* (young) in a particular pattern. His experiments growing pea plants led to the study of **genes.** Mendel's research explained how traits are passed down from one generation to another. His studies helped farmers improve the process of breeding plants and animals for stronger crops and livestock.

1866

Agriculture and the Industrial Revolution
1765—Late 1800's

New science and technology helped improve farming practices and made transporting crops easier. Such advances included the development of methods to safely store food for longer amounts of time. During the 1800's, canning factories opened in the United States. Many types of food, such as meats, fruits, and vegetables, could be safely packed into cans and transported over long distances. These canned foods were safe to eat for several years.

In the 1800's, *manufacturers* (people who processed foods in factories) also began freezing meats. By around 1880, fish was frozen and sold in the U.S. and

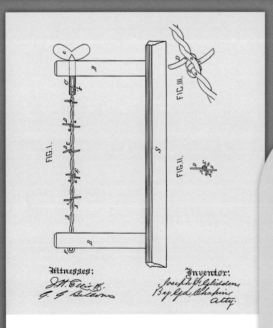

American Anna Baldwin created the first suction milking machine for cows. It was not successful because it pulled on the cow's udder, making the cow kick. But this device laid the basis for more successful milking machines in the future.

1879

1889

Italian Raffaele Esposito invented pizza as we know it today in Naples, Italy. He topped flatbread with tomato sauce, mozzarella cheese, and basil, which formed the colors of the Italian flag. Today, this type of pizza is called *Margherita* because Esposito served it to Queen Margherita of Savoy during a state visit in 1889.

American Joseph F. Glidden (1813-1906), a resident of the state of Illinois in the United States, invented barbed wire to use for fencing land. This type of fence allowed farmers to contain their livestock in one outdoor area.

1874

Europe. Australian companies began freezing beef in the 1870's. People in New Zealand froze *mutton* (sheep meat) and **exported** it to other lands.

Despite these improvements, some people throughout the world endured **famine** and hunger. Europeans had *colonized* (taken control of) many Asian and African countries, sometimes forcing people living in these nations to work on large farms. The crops were then sent to wealthy European countries, leaving little food for local people. Some areas of Europe, such as the modern country of Ireland, were also colonized. During the Great Irish Famine (1845-1850) about 1 million Irish people starved to death because the potato crop failed, while successful crops were shipped elsewhere to be sold. Many other people left Ireland to start a new life in such countries as Canada, the United States, or Australia.

American farmer John Froelich (1849-1933), a resident of the state of Iowa in the United States, developed the first gasoline-powered tractor. He attached it to a threshing machine, which separated the grains of the wheat crop from the stalks. Over time, many improvements were made to the tractor, but its basic design is largely the same today. The tractor is one of the most important pieces of farm machinery.

1892

1895

A major **drought** hit most of Australia in 1895 and continued until 1903. During this drought, Australians developed new kinds of wheat that could better survive dry conditions.

Chapter 6

The Influence of Industry
Early 1900's—Mid-1950's

By the 1900's, many countries were using industrial farming technology. Using mechanical tools and advanced planting methods, farmers could increase **yields.** Farmers used new agricultural machines to speed up tasks. But new machines were just a part of the advancements. By the 1900's, farmers had gained knowledge on **fertilizing** plants. Soon, farmers could help plants grow larger and faster by applying factory-made chemicals to the soil.

Swedish engineer Carl Gustav de Laval (1845-1913) invented the first successful milking machine for cattle. The machine was not manufactured until five years after his death.

1918

German chemist Fritz Haber (1868-1934) invented a process to make ammonia gas. Ammonia, in turn, is used to make nitrogen fertilizer, the most widely used kind.

1909

British scientist Frederick Hopkins (1861-1947, left) discovered that healthy people need small amounts of substances in foods called *vitamins*. Hopkins separated these substances from the "basic food factors"— carbohydrates, fats, proteins, minerals, and water. Polish scientist Casimir Funk (1884-1967) coined the word *vitamin* in 1912.

1906

In the past, farmers had used natural fertilizers, including *manure* (animal waste) and rotting plants. By the 1900's, scientists had discovered how to make *artificial* (human-made) fertilizers from chemicals in oils and gases. Now farmers did not need to rely on a limited supply of natural fertilizer. They could buy as much artificial fertilizer as they needed.

Other new chemicals, called **pesticides,** protected crops by poisoning pests and weeds that caused crops to fail. Farmers also introduced **hormones,** substances that make animals grow bigger and stronger, to livestock. *Antibiotics* (substances that prevent the growth of **bacteria**) are given to some types of farm animals to control disease. Though these chemicals help plants and animals grow, they can also damage the environment.

1920's

All-purpose tractors, powered by gasoline engines, were developed. They could pull almost any kind of farm equipment.

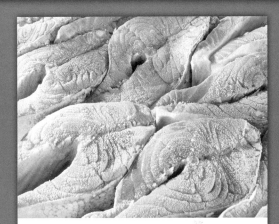

American food pioneer Clarence Birdseye (1886-1956) improved the method of freezing and packaging fish. After watching fishermen in the Canadian Arctic, he noticed that rapidly freezing fish after it was caught caused little damage to the food. Birdseye first marketed quick-frozen fish in 1925.

1925

1928

Collective, or shared, state-owned farms began in the Soviet Union.

27

The Influence of Industry
Early 1900's—Mid-1950's

In 1953, scientists discovered **DNA,** a chainlike structure found in every living thing. DNA is made up of **genes.** Genes control the traits or characteristics—such as height or eye color—in each living thing. The science of genetics helped people develop **hybrid** plants. A hybrid plant is a cross between two related plants; the useful traits from each plant are combined in the hybrid. The first hybrid plants developed in the 1900's included hybrid corn. This crop produced a high **yield.** By the 1960's, hybrid corn made up 95 percent of all corn grown in the U.S.

The development of new industries in the U.S. and Europe increased the range

The U.S. Food and Drug Administration (FDA) was established. This agency inspects the foods and medicines available for sale to protect public health. Other developed countries also established similar agencies.

American businessman Michael J. Cullen (1884-1936) opened the world's first supermarket in Queens, a borough of New York City. It revolutionized the grocery business. Cullen's huge self-service store allowed customers to purchase a variety of products under one roof. He sold both natural and processed foods. (All canned, dried, frozen, and pickled foods are processed.) Packaged frozen food became popular in the 1940's, when refrigerators and freezers became more common in private homes.

The **pesticide** DDT was first used to kill weeds that threatened crops.

1930

1930

Mid-1940's

1941

The United States Food and Nutrition Board of the National Academy of Sciences published the first Recommended Dietary Allowances (RDA's). RDA's are estimated amounts of various **nutrients** people need to consume daily to maintain good health.

of processed foods for sale. Advances in technology allowed such foods as meat, milk, and flour to be processed before they reached the grocery store. Such processed foods as frozen meals, potato chips, crackers, breakfast cereals, and ice cream became popular. Food processing also made fast-food restaurants possible in **developed countries.**

At this time in the Soviet Union and China, **agriculture** developed in a different way. These countries created huge *collective* (shared) farms. The government often owned these farms and hoped to speed up industrial development. But the government did not run the farms well, and most farmers did not like the government's tight control. In both countries, food production fell sharply, leading to terrible **famines.**

The United Kingdom established a law that required milk to be pasteurized before it is sold. Pasteurization is the use of heat to kill **bacteria** in foods. Louis Pasteur (1822-1895) of France invented this food safety method in the 1850's.

1949

1955

American businessman Ray Kroc (1902-1984) bought the hamburger restaurant McDonald's. He turned the company into a franchise. In a franchise, many restaurants use the same name and sell the same foods. People liked that all McDonald's restaurants had low prices, and its food tasted the same at all of its locations. Soon afterward, many other fast food restaurants used the franchise model. Fast food soon became extremely popular in the U.S. and other developed countries.

1958

Collective agriculture practices began in China.

Chapter 7

The Green Revolution
Late 1950's—1970

In the mid-1900's, U.S. and European scientists helped spread the techniques and technologies of industrialized **agriculture** to less **developed countries** in Asia, Africa, and Central and South America. This expansion became known as the *Green Revolution.* Such new types of **hybrid** plants as corn, wheat, and rice grew quickly and produced large **yields.**

During this time, food production rapidly increased, especially in Asia and

Supermarkets became the most popular place to buy food in the United States and United Kingdom. Supermarkets offered a wide range of fresh, frozen, canned, and other processed foods. Today's supermarkets often belong to chain stores. Some supermarkets are commonly called "big box" stores. In addition to groceries, these huge stores offer an even wider selection of goods for sale, including clothing, furniture, and medications.

Astronaut John Glenn (1921-   ) was the first American to eat food in outer space. The first foods developed for space travel included bite-sized cubes, powders, and semiliquids in squeeze tubes. Today's space-travel foods are mainly freeze-dried on Earth and then reheated with hot water in the spacecraft.

1962

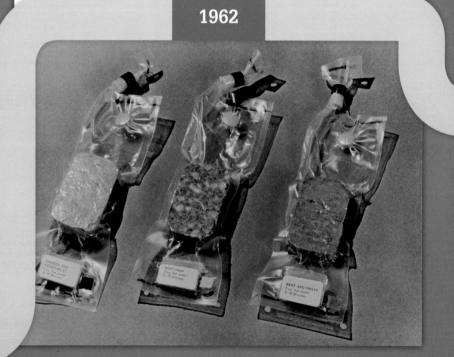

Late 1950's

South America. Many people were saved from starvation. But there were some disadvantages. To increase crops, farmers used chemical **fertilizers** and **pesticides.** They grew crops as monocultures—growing just one crop on large areas of land rather than planting a variety of foods. These practices damaged the environment. In addition, some of the poorest farmers could not afford the new technology, so they eventually lost their farms. The Green Revolution made little improvement to agriculture in Africa.

Successful farming also depended upon a nation's ability to organize agricultural methods in effective ways. After China's long-time leader Mao Zedong died in 1976, the government slowly ended its collective farming rules. The Chinese government allowed people to own land again, and food production increased.

American scientist Norman Borlaug (1914–2009) won the Nobel Peace Prize for developing high-yielding types of wheat. During the 1960's, such countries as India and Pakistan had planted these varieties. They were able to feed their populations and grow extra grain for **export.**

1970

1966

The United States government passed the Fair Packaging and Labeling Act. This act required the package used for a food product to contain such information as the manufacturer's information and the identification of the type of food in the product. Later, food labels included a freshness date, nutritional information, and complete list of ingredients, including chemical substances.

1962

American scientist Rachel Carson (1907–1964) wrote *Silent Spring.* She explained that pesticides used on crops poison the food supply of both humans and wild animals. Her arguments helped lead many countries to place limits on the use of farming pesticides. In the 1970's, the U.S. banned the use of the pesticide DDT.

Chapter 8

Feeding Our World
1973—Today

By the 1980's, some people worried that industrialized farming had grown too large to continue—it had become *unsustainable.* They believed that farming had damaged the environment so much that a change in farming practices was needed. Modern farms can strip an area's soil of its **nutrients.** Some **irrigated** farms use far more water than can be replaced by rainfall. Beginning in the 1980's, scientists began work on new **sustainable** methods to provide enough food for the world's people without depleting resources and destroying the environment.

Brazil launched a program to make an *ethanol* (alcohol) biofuel from sugar cane. The country was the world's largest biofuel producer until the United States overtook it in 2006.

1975

1976

The U.S. passed the Magnuson-Stevens Fishery Conservation and Management Act. This act helps to prevent overfishing—catching so many fish that not enough survive to create later generations. The act promotes long-term sustainable fishing practices. Many countries passed similar laws in the 1970's.

1973

Scientists learned how to change a living thing's **genes** directly through their **DNA.** Before this time, people could create new varieties of crops and livestock only by breeding them, using genetics as a guide. By altering or adding genes directly in DNA, scientists could give living things useful new features. For example, a gene might help a plant to resist insects or drought. This process of altering genes is called *genetic engineering*.

Like other modern industries, farming uses much oil and gas to power machines. Scientists believe that burning such natural fuels traps heat in Earth's atmosphere, causing **climate change.** By the early 2000's, for example, eastern Africa was suffering long **droughts** and western Africa endured floods. If Earth's climate continues to change, farmers around the world will likely need to learn new **agricultural** methods.

As countries have become more developed, the demand for meat has increased. Farmers grow such crops as corn to feed to their livestock instead of growing crops for people to eat. Producing biofuels also causes a decrease in the human food supply. Biofuel comes from crops grown for their sugar, including corn. These crops can be made into gasoline, but this leaves less food for people to eat.

China's government gradually ended state-run farming collectives.

1979   1988

The United Nations and the World Meteorological Organization set up the Intergovernmental Panel on Climate Change (IPCC). The panel gathers scientific information about Earth's changing climate. It has found that industrialized agriculture is a major factor in global warming. The panel has also warned that climate change will have major effects on agriculture around the world.

1988

The fair trade movement began. The movement attempts to ensure that farmers around the world receive fair prices for their foods so they can earn a decent living and feed their families. In return, the producers agree to farm in sustainable ways that help protect the environment and farm workers.

Feeding Our World
1973—Today

By the early 2000's, farms had spread dramatically to cover about 40 percent of Earth's surface. **Genetically modified (GM)** foods are among the most debated new technologies in **agriculture.** In a GM crop, certain **genes** are inserted directly into the **DNA** of the plant. These genes give the plant useful features, including disease-resistance or hardy grain kernels. Most of the corn and soybeans grown in the United States today are GM crops. But many people worry about environmental risks from GM crops.

Not all farmers use industrial techniques or GM seeds. Some farms meet certain

The Soviet Union fell. A newly formed country, Russia, began breaking up the government-run collective farms.

The first Food Guide Pyramid was published in the U.S. The pyramid's shape and colors called attention to the recommended amounts of each of the major food groups that make up a healthy diet. The USDA replaced the pyramid in 2011 with the MyPlate symbol (below). This symbol is combined with dietary guidelines to encourage people to eat in healthy ways and make better food choices.

1991

1992

1996

1990

The U.S. government passed the Organic Foods Production Act to create standards for organic food production. The USDA certifies farms that meet such standards.

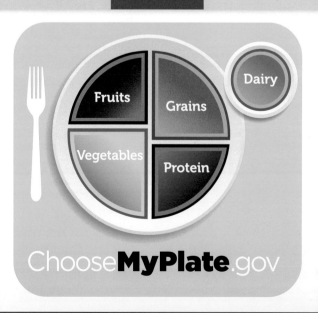

Monsanto, an agricultural company, produced Roundup-Ready, the first GM soybeans. Roundup is a type of pesticide Monsanto invented. The GM soybeans were especially designed to survive the Roundup pesticide, which killed all the weeds around the crops.

governmental standards and call their foods *organic.* Farms that produce organic foods do not use artificial **fertilizers** or **pesticides** on their plants. Organic livestock must be treated more humanely. Organic foods cannot be genetically modified. Though some people believe organic food is less harmful to the planet, it is often more expensive than industrially produced food.

Some industrial and organic farmers have turned to other **sustainable** methods of agriculture. These farms only raise crops that grow well in the local climate and do not need extra **irrigation.** These farmers use **crop rotation** to reduce fertilizer use. To limit the use of nonrenewable fuels in transportation, some farmers sell their foods at local farmers' markets.

Many bees in the United States and other countries began suddenly dying. The die-off became known as *colony collapse disorder.* Scientists thought that disease, *parasites* (tiny creatures living on the bees), or the use of pesticides caused the die-offs. The death of bees hurts the agriculture industry. Farmers depend on bees not only for their honey but also to pollinate plants grown for food. Pollination is the movement of pollen between male and female parts of plants to make new plants.

2004

2006

Golden Rice was first harvested in the U.S. and was later grown in less **developed countries.** This GM crop contained Vitamin A, which helps prevent blindness. People in parts of Africa and India especially benefited from such a boost in Vitamin A.

Feeding Our World
1973—Today

Feeding the world's people in the future depends on modern farming techniques and the organization of society. In wealthy **developed countries,** many people eat too much food, especially unhealthy fast food and snacks. This unbalanced diet can lead to *obesity,* or an unhealthy body weight. However, many other people have the opposite problem—they do not have enough to eat. In the 2010's, nearly a billion people worldwide suffered from hunger and starvation. Many of these people lived in less developed countries without much access to the modern food supply. But some people living in more developed countries also are not able to

2011

Thirty percent of adults over 20 years of age worldwide were considered overweight or obese.

2012

2008

Food prices increased sharply around the world, especially prices for **staple** grains. Causes for the high prices included **droughts,** high oil prices, increased demand for meat, and biofuel production.

In New York City, hundreds of fast-food workers went on strike. They demanded higher wages. The movement spread across the world.

get enough food. Both obesity and starvation are extreme forms of *malnutrition* (a poor or inappropriate diet).

Agriculture continues to be the world's most important industry. In the early 2000's, farmers produced more than enough food for the world's population of more than 7 billion people. Agriculture provides materials for clothing, shelter, medicine, fuels, plants, and other goods. The challenge lies in ensuring that everyone has access to the food supply. Another challenge involves making the food supply more **sustainable** so it does not cause lasting harm to the environment. In the future, finding solutions to agricultural needs will be necessary to continue to feed people throughout the world.

U.S. First Lady Michelle Obama's *Let's Move!* campaign celebrated its fifth anniversary. This governmental program aims to reduce childhood obesity through healthful eating habits and daily exercise.

2015   **2016**

2013

Food researchers grew beef in a scientific laboratory from the cells of cows. The meat was made into a hamburger. Taste testers sampled the flavor of the artificial meat and thought it was acceptable.

The U.S. Health and Human Services Department announced the 2015–2020 Dietary Guidelines for Americans. These guidelines focused on reducing sugar and salt in people's diets.

Glossary

agriculture   the farming of plants and animals for human benefit.

bacteria   single-celled organisms that can only be seen using a microscope. Some bacteria cause disease.

climate change   changes to Earth caused by global warming. The warming is due to the increase of particular gases, especially carbon dioxide given off by human activities.

crop rotation   a system of planting an area of land with different crops each growing season.

developed country   a country with many industries and a complex economic system.

DNA   short for *deoxyribonucleic acid*; the chainlike structure found in cells that carries genetic information and passes on features from parents to child.

domestication   changing, over time, wild animals and plants so as to make them suitable for agricultural purposes.

drought   a long period of time when there is little or no rain.

environment   everything on Earth—the air, water, soil, and plants—that makes up the surroundings of a living thing.

export   to sell goods to other countries.

famine   a lack of food for a long period of time.

fertilizer   a product that is added to soil or water to help plants to grow. It may be natural or human-made.

gene   a part of a cell that determines which characteristics living things inherit from their parents.

genetically modified (GM) crops   crops with *genes* (hereditary material) that have been altered directly. Such genes may help crops grow faster or make them better able to resist disease.

hormone   a chemical substance produced in the body that encourages growth or influences how cells function.

hybrid   offspring of animals or plants of different varieties.

import   to buy goods from other countries.

irrigation   to supply water to an area of land through pipes or channels to help crops to grow.

Middle Ages   the period in European history between ancient and modern times, from about the A.D. 400's through about the 1400's. The end date depends on the region of Europe considered.

nutrient   a nourishing substance needed to keep a living thing alive and healthy.

pesticide   a chemical used to kill bacteria, insects, or other living things that damage plants.

preserve   to treat or change food so it lasts longer.

staple crop   a crop that serves as the main food people eat. Wheat, rice, and such starchy *tubers* (root plants) as potatoes are examples of staple crops.

sustainable agriculture   methods of raising crops and livestock in ways that reduce long-term environmental damage from farming.

yield   the total amount produced.

Find Out More

Books

The 12 Biggest Breakthroughs in Food Technology by Marne Ventura (12-Story Library, 2015)

Cycle of Rice, Cycle of Life by Jan Reynolds (Lee & Low Books, 2009)

The Dish on Food and Farming in Colonial America by Anika Fajardo (Capstone Press, 2012)

Food: 25 Amazing Projects Investigate the History and Science of What We Eat by Kathleen M. Reilly (Nomad Press, 2010)

Food For Thought: The Stories Behind the Things We Eat by Ken Robbins (Roaring Brook Press, 2009)

Inventors of Food and Agriculture Technology by Heather Morrison (Cavendish Square Publishing, 2015)

Who Wants Pizza? The Kids' Guide to the History, Science and Culture of Food by Jan Thornhill (Owlkids Books, 2010)

Websites

BBC Primary History – Indus Valley: Food and Farming
http://www.bbc.co.uk/schools/primaryhistory/indus_valley/food_and_farming/
See photos, play games, and learn fun facts about the food and farming practices of the Indus Valley civilization.

Growing a Nation – Historical Timeline: Farm Machinery & Technology
https://www.agclassroom.org/gan/timeline/farm_tech.htm
View a historical timeline showing the development of farm machinery and technology in the United States.

My American Farm
http://www.myamericanfarm.org/classroom/games
Play interactive games about agriculture while practicing math, science, and social studies skills.

National Agriculture in the Classroom – Kids' Zone
http://www.agclassroom.org/kids/index.htm
Explore virtual tours of real farms, select a science fair project, or learn about agricultural practices in each state.

National Geographic Education – Agriculture
http://education.nationalgeographic.com/encyclopedia/agriculture/
Learn more about the world of agriculture with an informative article, leveled activities, and historical photos.

NeoK12 – Agriculture
http://www.neok12.com/Agriculture.htm
Watch dozens of educational videos that identify and discuss key moments the history of agriculture.

Index